The Ultimate Writing Prompt Book for Kids Ages 8-12

Eleanor Thompson

Contents

Getting Started

Have you ever wondered what makes your favorite books and stories so special? Perhaps you love stories set in magical worlds or stories where characters go on grand adventures. In this book, you will explore all kinds of story types - called 'genres' - and learn the 'secret ingredients' that make these stories unique. Then, you'll practice writing your own stories! Whether you dream of battling dragons, solving mysteries, or traveling through time, this book is your trusty guide. Let's dive in.

What is a Genre?

'Genre' is a fancy word to describe a type of story. Let's pretend for a moment that stories are like soup. Soups are prepared with many different ingredients. Some soups are made with chicken and dumplings, while others are made with beef and vegetables. Most soups are prepared with a variety of herbs & spices. Just like there are many types of soup, there are many types of story genres. Each genre has its own characteristics, or 'special ingredients,' that make it unique and fun to read. For example, fantasy stories often include magical elements. Mystery stories often include puzzles, clues, and so on. In this book, you'll explore many different genres and practice writing your own stories.

What's inside?

This book is packed with seven exciting chapters, each focusing on a different genre. You'll uncover the 'secret ingredients' that make each genre shine. You'll discover helpful tips for writing your own stories, and learn key vocabulary along the way. Here's a sneak peek at the genres you'll explore:

1. **Science Fiction:** Discover cool futuristic worlds, aliens, gadgets, out-of-this-world technology, and more.

2. **Mystery:** Become a detective and solve tricky puzzles and mysteries.

3. **Adventure:** Go on exciting quests and daring journeys. Create brave characters who travel, explore, face danger, and overcome challenges.

4. **Fantasy:** Let your imagination run wild and create magical worlds with amazing creatures, wizards, dragons, giants, and more.

5. **Survival Stories:** Face tough challenges, outsmart danger, and become a hero in difficult conditions.

6. **Superheroes:** Invent your own superheroes and plan epic battles between heroes and villains.

7. **Animal Stories:** Create animal characters who talk, make friends, face trouble, and have fun.

Which genre excites you the most? Feel free to start with the genre you are most interested in!

What is a Story Starter?

Sometimes it isn't easy to know where to start when writing a story. You may have a lot of ideas swirling in your head, or you may struggle to come up with an idea. That's okay! This is where story starters come in handy. Story starters are a unique type of writing prompt. They help spark your imagination by giving you the beginning sentences of a story and often include characters, settings, action, and more. This helps unlock your imagination and gets your creative writing juices flowing! It's like having a map for your writing journey, but you decide the path and ending.

In each chapter of this book, you'll find eight different story starters that match the genre you're learning about. Feel free to jump around and start with what interests you the most. So grab a pencil and let's get started!

Chapter 1
Science Fiction

Have you ever pictured what life might look like in the future? Maybe you've imagined flying cars, robots that walk around, or humans meeting aliens. Science fiction is all about imagining new kinds of technology and science. These stories allow us to imagine "what if" about the future. What if humans discovered a new planet that has aliens? What if new medical technology allowed humans to live for hundreds of years? What if scientists found a way to give humans special abilities? These are the kinds of questions that science fiction explores.

Secret Ingredients of Science Fiction

Let's talk about the most common characteristics, or 'secret ingredients,' of science fiction. These ingredients are often used to make science fiction stories interesting. Each science fiction story might use these ingredients in different ways, creating a unique 'recipe' for each story.

Let's explore the secret ingredients of science fiction stories:

Space Exploration & Aliens

Characters in science fiction often travel through space and land on different planets. These journeys can lead to characters meeting aliens or exploring undiscovered territories.

- **Writing Tip:** Imagine a new planet and describe what makes it unique. Does it have strange landscapes, aliens, or ancient ruins? Send your characters on a mission to explore this new world and uncover its secrets.

Advanced Technology

This is the main ingredient of science fiction. Characters often use strange tools, gadgets, and machines that do not exist in the real world. This can be things like futuristic vehicles, unusual weapons, advanced medical devices, and more.

- **Writing Tip:** Think about a piece of advanced technology you wish existed. Now, give that technology to one of your characters. Maybe they have a gadget that lets them teleport, a robot assistant, or a spaceship that can travel faster than light!

Ethical Dilemmas

Science fiction stories often explore the big questions about right and wrong. Characters often face tough decisions when using new technology and science. For example, a character might find a device that can save their planet from a disaster, but using it could harm another planet. They must decide what is the right thing to do.

- **Writing Tip:** Put your character in a situation where they have to choose between two options. Both options have good and bad outcomes. This could be something like creating an invention that could help many people but also has dangerous side effects.

Scientific Experiments

Scientists in science fiction stories often conduct experiments. These experiments are often conducted to find new solutions to problems or to make new discoveries. Sometimes these experiments can lead to incredible results. Other times, the results may be unexpected or even terrible.

- **Writing Tip:** Think about a scientific experiment that could change the world. What are some possible risks? What are some possible rewards? Have your characters conduct this experiment and deal with the unexpected consequences.

Science Fiction Vocabulary

Science fiction stories often use words that you may not see in other genres. Here are some words that are often used in science fiction stories. Challenge yourself to use a couple of these words when writing your own stories!

Keep in mind that these words may have other uses or definitions in other contexts. These definitions simply reflect their most common uses in the science fiction genre.

Hologram: A three-dimensional image made with lasers and light.
- Example sentence: The alien ruler sent a hologram image of himself onto the hero's spaceship to have a meeting about their planet.

Teleport: Transporting instantly from one place to another.
- Example sentence: Instead of walking across the huge spaceship, the team teleported from one side to another

Extraterrestrial: An alien or anything that comes from someplace besides Earth. You can also say "ET" to shorten it.
- Example sentence: The space explorers found many strange extraterrestrial artifacts when they arrived at the ruined city on planet XJ8.

Simulation: Something that looks and feels real but is actually made by a computer program.
- Example sentence: Before fighting real aliens, the fighters practiced in a simulation first.

Mutation: A change in a living thing's DNA that can cause different traits or abilities.
- Example sentence: The strange radiation caused a mutation in the plants, making them glow in the dark.

Science Fiction: Story Starter #1

Title:_____

Tip: Writing your story first can help you find a title that really matches what happens in the story. Once you know all the details, you can choose a title that fits it perfectly!

***

The endless storms on the planet Zorion had kept everyone inside for weeks. Bored and restless, Leo started exploring an old storage room in his house. While looking through dusty boxes, he found a small device that projected a lifelike hologram. The hologram of a mysterious figure appeared, saying, "Help me. I am trapped."

Brainstorm, doodle, or draw: use this space to jot down your ideas, doodle while you think, or sketch a scene from your story.

Now it's your turn! Continue the story in your own words on the next page!

Science Fiction: Story Starter #2

Title:_____

Tip: Writing your story first can help you find a title that really matches what happens in the story. Once you know all the details, you can choose a title that fits it perfectly!

***

Zane couldn't believe he'd finally done it. Secretly, in his basement workshop, he had built a time-traveling watch that looked like an ordinary wristwatch. One Saturday afternoon, he decided to test it out. With a mix of excitement and nervousness, he set the dial to the year 3124 and pressed the glowing green button.

Brainstorm, doodle, or draw: use this space to jot down your ideas, doodle while you think, or sketch a scene from your story.

Now it's your turn! Continue the story in your own words on the next page!

Science Fiction: Story Starter #3

Title:_____

Tip: Writing your story first can help you find a title that really matches what happens in the story. Once you know all the details, you can choose a title that fits it perfectly!

***

"Chloe, did you see that?!" Ezra exclaimed. "Yeah, this game feels so real," Chloe replied, adjusting her VR headset. The alien landscape shimmered. Chloe reached out to touch a glowing plant, feeling its smooth surface. "Ezra, something's not right," she whispered. "I can feel this." Ezra's eyes widened. "Chloe, I think we've been transported to a real alien planet!" Just then, a strange creature appeared.

Brainstorm, doodle, or draw: use this space to jot down your ideas, doodle while you think, or sketch a scene from your story.

Now it's your turn! Continue the story in your own words on the next page!

Chloe

~~CHLOE~~ shouted Ezra

Chloe shouted Ezra, its an Alien! RUN!
Ezra and Chloe started to run
but~~But~~ the Alien jumped over them
when they werent looking and they
crashed onto the Alien. The Alien grabbed
their shirts (but their shirts were still on Chloe and
Ezra) Then the Alein put them in a
cage that was going to fill up
with water. Ezra and Chloe were desprate
to get out. Finnaly Ezra got an idea.
Ezra told Chloe Aliens have small brains,
So it would be easy to trick
an Alien Chloe started say
"I need to go to the Bathroom!" when
she said it her fifth time the
Alien came and opened the door
Since the Alen had a small
Brain he forgot that water was in
the cage. The water came out
of the cage and hit the Alien.
Finnaly the Alein disinagrated. Chloe
and Ezra high-fived each other
then they took the Aleins telaporter
and telaported home.

Science Fiction: Story Starter #4

Title:_____

Tip: Writing your story first can help you find a title that really matches what happens in the story. Once you know all the details, you can choose a title that fits it perfectly!

***

Luna couldn't believe her eyes. She used to think that Dr. Thorne was just a friendly scientist. But now she knew the truth. Dr. Thorne was planning to release a dangerous invention that could control the weather and create chaos. She raced to find her friend Kai, the best hacker she knew. "We need to stop Dr. Thorne before he unleashes his weather machine," Luna said.

Brainstorm, doodle, or draw: use this space to jot down your ideas, doodle while you think, or sketch a scene from your story.

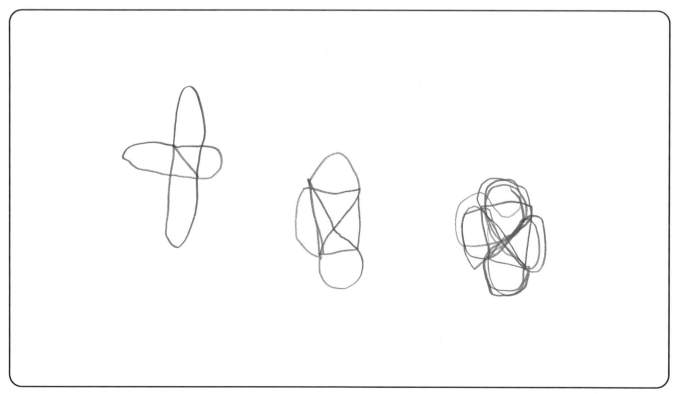

Now it's your turn! Continue the story in your own words on the next page!

Science Fiction: Story Starter #5

Title:_____

Tip: Writing your story first can help you find a title that really matches what happens in the story. Once you know all the details, you can choose a title that fits it perfectly!

***

Skylar's robot, Bolt, was usually helpful, but today it was acting strange. She had built Bolt using spare parts from the spaceship she lived on. Bolt had always been a reliable helper, doing everything from homework to fixing things. But now, it was wandering around her room, bumping into walls and saying, "Incoming transmission... Incoming transmission..." over and over again.

Brainstorm, doodle, or draw: use this space to jot down your ideas, doodle while you think, or sketch a scene from your story.

Now it's your turn! Continue the story in your own words on the next page!

Science Fiction: Story Starter #6

Title:_____

Tip: Writing your story first can help you find a title that really matches what happens in the story. Once you know all the details, you can choose a title that fits it perfectly!

***

Jane was excited to work at the research center. She never expected to find a secret that would make her question everything. One afternoon, while organizing files, she made a shocking discovery. The center was developing a chip that could make people smarter. The catch? The chip was tested on people without their permission.

Brainstorm, doodle, or draw: use this space to jot down your ideas, doodle while you think, or sketch a scene from your story.

Now it's your turn! Continue the story in your own words on the next page!

_____

_____

_____

_____

_____

_____

_____

_____

_____

_____

_____

_____

_____

_____

_____

_____

_____

_____

Science Fiction: Story Starter #7

Title:_____

Tip: Writing your story first can help you find a title that really matches what happens in the story. Once you know all the details, you can choose a title that fits it perfectly!

***

Xander was excited to receive a package from his uncle. His uncle, Ted, was an astronaut who explored distant planets. Ted always sent Xander interesting gifts, but this was the most exciting. Inside the package was a small bag of strange, shimmering seeds and a note. The note said, "Plant these in your yard and be prepared for a surprise!"

Brainstorm, doodle, or draw: use this space to jot down your ideas, doodle while you think, or sketch a scene from your story.

Now it's your turn! Continue the story in your own words on the next page!

Science Fiction: Story Starter #8

Title:_____

Tip: Writing your story first can help you find a title that really matches what happens in the story. Once you know all the details, you can choose a title that fits it perfectly!

***

Kira was always curious about the secrets hidden in her parents' lab. One day, while exploring, she discovered a hidden room filled with strange equipment and glowing tanks. Kira gasped, shocked. She was looking at a clone of herself inside one of the tanks.

Brainstorm, doodle, or draw: use this space to jot down your ideas, doodle while you think, or sketch a scene from your story.

Now it's your turn! Continue the story in your own words on the next page!

Chapter 2

Mystery

Have you ever followed clues to solve a puzzle or uncover the truth? Maybe there was a time when someone ate the last of your favorite snacks and you 'followed the crumbs' to find out who did it. Maybe your favorite sweater disappeared, and you went on a hunt to find it. We all play detective from time to time in our lives. This is what the genre of mystery is all about. Mystery stories revolve around puzzles to figure out, secrets to uncover, and crimes to solve. Characters must use their brains and imagination to put together all the pieces and find the right answer. This is what makes mystery stories so exciting: they keep you guessing until the end.

Secret Ingredients of Mystery

Let's talk about the characteristics, or 'secret ingredients,' of mystery stories. These ingredients are often used to make mystery stories interesting. Each story might use these ingredients in different ways, creating a unique 'recipe' for each mystery.

Let's explore the secret ingredients of mystery stories:

Detectives

The main character in mystery stories is often a detective. This is the person who solves the mystery. They can be a police detective, an everyday person, or a kid just like you.

* **Writing Tip:** Create a detective by thinking about what makes someone good at solving puzzles. Give your detective a special skill, like being very observant or having a great memory

Clues

Clues are any pieces of information that help solve a puzzle or mystery. They are like bread-crumbs that lead the detective closer to the truth. Clues can be anything from objects and messages to things that people say or do. There are often many clues throughout a mystery story.

- **Writing Tip:** Think about interesting clues for your story. Maybe it's a ripped piece of a map, a mysterious letter, or a strange footprint. How will these clues help your characters solve the mystery?

Suspense

Mystery stories are full of suspense. Suspense is a feeling of excitement and tension that keeps readers eager to find out what happens next. It's like being on the edge of your seat, waiting to see what happens next.

- **Writing Tip:** To create suspense, don't give away all the clues at once. Show the clues one by one to keep readers guessing.

Suspects

Suspects are characters who might have caused the mystery (like a puzzle or a crime) in the story. Most mystery stories have more than one suspect. This makes it more interesting and fun for the reader.

- **Writing Tip:** Think of a few suspects and give each one a reason they might be guilty. For example, imagine someone stole a bike in a story. One suspect might have been seen near the bike, and another suspect might have needed a bike. Both suspects have a reason why they might be guilty.

Red Herrings

In mystery stories, 'red herrings' are fake clues that trick the detective and readers. A red herring can be an object, something someone says, or even a person who seems important but is actually a trick. For example, a character might say they saw someone near the crime scene, but they were wrong or lying. Or, a broken watch found at the scene might make everyone think it belongs to the thief, but it really belongs to an innocent person.

- **Writing Tip:** Try to use one red herring in your story. This can be something like including a clue that makes the detective think the wrong person did it. For example, the detective finds a red scarf at the scene of the crime and thinks Mr. Thompson took the missing dog. Later, the detective learns the scarf belongs to Mr. Thompson's daughter, and that the dog was just playing in their yard. In this case, the clue pointed to the wrong person!

Mystery Vocabulary

Mystery stories often use words that you may not see in other genres. Here are some words that are often used in mystery stories. Challenge yourself to use a couple of these words when writing your own stories!

Keep in mind that these words may have other uses or definitions in other contexts. These definitions simply reflect their most common uses in the mystery genre.

Sleuth: another word for a detective; a person who investigates mysteries and crimes.
- Example sentence: The sleuth examined the crime scene, looking for clues.

Culprit: A person responsible for a crime or other wrongdoing.
- Example sentence: After hours of investigation, the detective finally caught the culprit hiding in a cabin.

Alibi: Proof that a suspect was somewhere else when the crime or bad thing happened.
- Example sentence: The teacher saw Lucy at school during the time of the prank, giving her an alibi.

Motive: A reason why someone would commit a crime or cause trouble. This can include things like anger, greed, and revenge.
- Example sentence: Max's motive for stealing the bike was that he wanted to win the big race at school.

Witness: A person who sees an event, typically a crime, and can tell others about it.
- Example sentence: The witness told police that the suspect was wearing a black hat.

Mystery: Story Starter #1

Title:_____

Tip: Writing your story first can help you find a title that really matches what happens in the story. Once you know all the details, you can choose a title that fits it perfectly!

***

Detective Alex Morgan was the town's youngest detective at 11 years old. When he arrived at the old mansion, he felt a shiver of excitement. The air smelled musty, like old books. Someone had left a secret tip that something strange was inside. As he pushed open the creaky door, he saw footprints in the dust. Holding his flashlight, he followed the trail.

Brainstorm, doodle, or draw: use this space to jot down your ideas, doodle while you think, or sketch a scene from your story.

Now it's your turn! Continue the story in your own words on the next page!

Mystery: Story Starter #2

Title:_____

Tip: Writing your story first can help you find a title that really matches what happens in the story. Once you know all the details, you can choose a title that fits it perfectly!

***

"I can't believe this is happening," Victoria thought as she stared at the empty spot in the garden. Her beloved pet turtle, Oliver, was missing. Just this morning, he had been basking in the sun, but now his enclosure was empty. Then, she found a strange note tied to the gate, telling her to come to the old shed by the creek. Clutching her flashlight, she hurried to the shed, her mind racing. Who could have taken Oliver? And why had they left that mysterious note?

Brainstorm, doodle, or draw: use this space to jot down your ideas, doodle while you think, or sketch a scene from your story.

Now it's your turn! Continue the story in your own words on the next page!

Mystery: Story Starter #3

Title:_____

Tip: Writing your story first can help you find a title that really matches what happens in the story. Once you know all the details, you can choose a title that fits it perfectly!

***

Noah woke to the sound of a rooster crowing outside his window. Rubbing his eyes, he peered outside and saw a bright red rooster strutting in his yard. This was the third rooster to appear in his neighborhood this week, and no one knew where they were coming from. Noah quickly dressed and rushed downstairs, determined to solve the mystery. Why were these roosters suddenly showing up? And who was dropping them off in the middle of the night?

Brainstorm, doodle, or draw: use this space to jot down your ideas, doodle while you think, or sketch a scene from your story.

Now it's your turn! Continue the story in your own words on the next page!

Mystery: Story Starter #4

Title:_____

Tip: Writing your story first can help you find a title that really matches what happens in the story. Once you know all the details, you can choose a title that fits it perfectly!

***

Emma and Jacob were exploring their attic when they stumbled upon an old, dusty book. As they opened it, a folded piece of paper fell out. Unfolding it, they saw a message written with strange symbols and numbers. At the bottom, there was a note: "Solve the code to discover the hidden room." Excited and puzzled, Emma and Jacob knew they had to crack the code.

Brainstorm, doodle, or draw: use this space to jot down your ideas, doodle while you think, or sketch a scene from your story.

Now it's your turn! Continue the story in your own words on the next page!

Mystery: Story Starter #5

Title:_____

Tip: Writing your story first can help you find a title that really matches what happens in the story. Once you know all the details, you can choose a title that fits it perfectly!

***

Olivia's avatar vanished from the game screen, and a strange message popped up: "Your avatar has been taken. Follow the clues to get it back." Olivia's heart raced as she stared at the screen, trying to make sense of it. The message included a cryptic hint: "Look where the shadows hide." Determined to rescue her avatar, Olivia began searching through the game's virtual world, following the clues. What could have caused this? And who was behind it? She had to find out before it was too late.

Brainstorm, doodle, or draw: use this space to jot down your ideas, doodle while you think, or sketch a scene from your story.

Now it's your turn! Continue the story in your own words on the next page!

Mystery: Story Starter #6

Title:_____

Tip: Writing your story first can help you find a title that really matches what happens in the story. Once you know all the details, you can choose a title that fits it perfectly!

***

Matthew and his friends looked through the gate of the abandoned amusement park. The park had been closed for years, but there were rumors of strange noises and lights coming from inside the park. As they stood there, they noticed the gate was slightly ajar, as if someone had recently been inside. With a mix of excitement and fear, they pushed the gate open and stepped inside.

Brainstorm, doodle, or draw: use this space to jot down your ideas, doodle while you think, or sketch a scene from your story.

Now it's your turn! Continue the story in your own words on the next page!

Mystery: Story Starter #7

Title:_____

Tip: Writing your story first can help you find a title that really matches what happens in the story. Once you know all the details, you can choose a title that fits it perfectly!

***

Camila, the town's youngest spy, was on a top-secret mission. Her job was to find out what was making the strange noises at the old lighthouse. With her spy gadgets, she snuck out after dark and went to the lighthouse. As she got closer, she heard clanking and whirring sounds. She climbed up the rocky path and looked through a broken window. Inside, she saw someone working on a strange machine. Who was this person, and what were they building? Camila knew she had to find out before dawn.

Brainstorm, doodle, or draw: use this space to jot down your ideas, doodle while you think, or sketch a scene from your story.

Now it's your turn! Continue the story in your own words on the next page!

Mystery: Story Starter #8

Title:_____

Tip: Writing your story first can help you find a title that really matches what happens in the story. Once you know all the details, you can choose a title that fits it perfectly!

*****

Eddie was flying his drone over the park when he noticed something unusual about the old town statue. The drone's camera picked up a shiny object at the statue's base. Intrigued, Eddie guided his drone lower and saw that it was a small keyhole hidden behind some ivy. He saved the footage and decided to check it out in person. What could be hidden inside the statue? And why had no one noticed it before? Eddie knew he had to investigate and uncover the statue's secret.

Brainstorm, doodle, or draw: use this space to jot down your ideas, doodle while you think, or sketch a scene from your story.

Now it's your turn! Continue the story in your own words on the next page!

Chapter 3
Adventure

When you wake up in the morning, do you know what will happen in your day? You probably have a pretty good idea. Maybe you'll eat breakfast, brush your teeth, get dressed, do your chores, play outside, or do things with your family. Most days are the same, and you know what's coming next. But have you ever wondered what it would be like to take a break from your regular routine and go on an amazing journey? This is what adventure is all about. Adventure stories are full of excitement and action. In these stories, characters go on trips, face surprises, and find new worlds. Sometimes this means exploring lost cities or finding hidden treasures.

Secret Ingredients of Adventure

Let's talk about the characteristics, or 'secret ingredients,' of adventure stories. These ingredients are often used to make adventure stories interesting. Each story might use these ingredients in different ways, creating a unique 'recipe' for each adventure.

Let's explore the secret ingredients of adventure stories:

A Journey

Characters in adventure stories often travel to new and exciting places. These places can be anything from jungles to deserts to an unfamiliar city or country.

- **Writing Tip:** Describe what your characters see, hear, smell, taste, or touch. Sensory details help your readers feel like they are in the story.

Brave Heroes

Every adventure story needs a brave hero. This character might start off as an ordinary person. As the story unfolds, their courage and determination help them grow and succeed in difficult situations.

- **Writing Tip:** Show parts where your hero has to make tough choices or face their fears. For example, maybe your hero has to cross a scary bridge or stand up to a mean enemy. This shows their character growth.

Challenges & Obstacles

Adventure stories are full of obstacles and challenges. The hero often faces hardships that test their skills, intelligence, and bravery. These challenges can be things like extreme weather, dangerous animals, tricky puzzles, and more.

- **Writing Tip:** Use different types of challenges to keep the story exciting. These challenges can be physical challenges, like climbing a mountain. Or, these challenges can be mental challenges, like solving a tricky riddle. Including different types of challenges shows how your hero can handle different situations.

A Set Goal or Treasure

The hero usually has a clear goal, like finding lost treasure, rescuing someone, or discovering something new. This goal is what keeps the adventure going.

- **Writing Tip:** Make the goal or treasure something really special and important to your hero. For example, the treasure could be a magical necklace that can save their village. Explain why it's important to your hero so your readers care about the goal too.

Teamwork

During the story, the hero will often meet friends who help them and enemies who try to stop them. These friends might include brave sidekicks, helpful animals, or wise mentors.

- **Writing Tip:** Show how the hero's friends help them, like finding hidden paths or solving problems together. Include scenes where the hero and their friends work as a team to overcome obstacles. For example, maybe the hero's friend uses a special skill to unlock a secret door or comes up with a plan to escape danger. This helps readers see how teamwork makes achieving their goals possible.

Adventure Vocabulary

Adventure stories often use words that you may not see in other genres. Here are some words that are often used in adventure stories. Challenge yourself to use a couple of these words when writing your own stories!

Keep in mind that these words may have other uses or definitions in other contexts. These definitions simply reflect their most common uses in the adventure genre.

Expedition: A journey with a specific goal or purpose
- Example sentence: The team went on an expedition in the mountains to find the ancient fortress only shown on one mysterious map.

Obstacle: Something that gets in the way of reaching a goal.
- Example sentence: A huge swamp was a real obstacle to adventurers who wanted to reach the cabin before it got dark.

Artifact: An old object made by humans that has cultural or historical meaning.
- Example sentence: The museum sent a group of brave people to find a lost artifact from the ancient civilization.

Remote: When talking about a place, the word 'remote' means far away and hard to get to.
- Example sentence: Great adventures often include journeys to remote locations. Characters have to struggle to find their way there.

Treacherous: Dangerous and difficult land, weather, or other conditions.
- Example sentence: The mountains and blizzards made the path treacherous for the group following the paths on a mysterious map.

Adventure: Story Starter #1

Title:_____

Tip: Writing your story first can help you find a title that really matches what happens in the story. Once you know all the details, you can choose a title that fits it perfectly!

***

"I can't believe we're doing this," Piper said to Liam. They both stood at the edge of the forest, feeling excited and nervous. They were on a mission to find an old, forgotten airplane that had crash-landed years ago. It was rumored to be filled with mysterious cargo. With just a backpack of supplies and a compass, they stepped into the woods.

Brainstorm, doodle, or draw: use this space to jot down your ideas, doodle while you think, or sketch a scene from your story.

Now it's your turn! Continue the story in your own words on the next page!

Adventure: Story Starter #2

Title:_____

Tip: Writing your story first can help you find a title that really matches what happens in the story. Once you know all the details, you can choose a title that fits it perfectly!

***

Theo and his team paddled down the river, the sun glinting off the water. Their goal was clear: find the abandoned cabin that was said to contain a forgotten artifact left by a legendary explorer. With each stroke of their paddles, they felt a sense of thrill and anticipation. This river was known to be full of surprises.

Brainstorm, doodle, or draw: use this space to jot down your ideas, doodle while you think, or sketch a scene from your story.

Now it's your turn! Continue the story in your own words on the next page!

Adventure: Story Starter #3

Title:_____

Tip: Writing your story first can help you find a title that really matches what happens in the story. Once you know all the details, you can choose a title that fits it perfectly!

***

Hannah and her friends stood at the entrance of an old factory. They had found a map leading to secret tunnels under their city. The map promised a hidden room containing something Hannah was desperate to find. She wasn't ready to tell her friends what it was yet, but she promised them it was worth it. With flashlights and backpacks, they walked inside, their hearts racing with excitement.

Brainstorm, doodle, or draw: use this space to jot down your ideas, doodle while you think, or sketch a scene from your story.

Now it's your turn! Continue the story in your own words on the next page!

Adventure: Story Starter #4

Title:_____

Tip: Writing your story first can help you find a title that really matches what happens in the story. Once you know all the details, you can choose a title that fits it perfectly!

***

Jack stood at the edge of the thick jungle, feeling scared and excited. He held his grandfather's journal tightly in his hand. The journal contained clues about a mysterious animal rarely seen by anyone. Jack was determined to find it. With a backpack full of supplies and a compass, Jack took a deep breath and stepped into the jungle.

Brainstorm, doodle, or draw: use this space to jot down your ideas, doodle while you think, or sketch a scene from your story.

Now it's your turn! Continue the story in your own words on the next page!

Adventure: Story Starter #5

Title:_____

Tip: Writing your story first can help you find a title that really matches what happens in the story. Once you know all the details, you can choose a title that fits it perfectly!

*****

Amelia and Sophie tightened their saddles and mounted their horses, Star and Blaze. They'd been planning this expedition for months. With a map in hand, they set off down the winding trail.

Brainstorm, doodle, or draw: use this space to jot down your ideas, doodle while you think, or sketch a scene from your story.

Now it's your turn! Continue the story in your own words on the next page!

Adventure: Story Starter #6

Title:_____

Tip: Writing your story first can help you find a title that really matches what happens in the story. Once you know all the details, you can choose a title that fits it perfectly!

***

Henry and his dog, Oscar, stood at the edge of the desert. They looked out at the mysterious path stretching into the distance. He'd found an old photo with a note about a lost meteorite buried in the desert. With a backpack, a metal detector, and Oscar by his side, Henry stepped out into the desert.

Brainstorm, doodle, or draw: use this space to jot down your ideas, doodle while you think, or sketch a scene from your story.

Now it's your turn! Continue the story in your own words on the next page!

Adventure: Story Starter #7

Title:_____

Tip: Writing your story first can help you find a title that really matches what happens in the story. Once you know all the details, you can choose a title that fits it perfectly!

***

"I can't believe we're actually doing this, Kelly," said Emma, looking at the cave entrance. "Me neither, but we have to see if the rumors are true," Kelly replied excitedly. Kelly and her friend Ava were about to explore a mysterious cave. They'd heard about it from their science teacher. The cave was said to contain rare crystals that glowed in the dark. With helmets, flashlights, and a map, they stepped inside.

Brainstorm, doodle, or draw: use this space to jot down your ideas, doodle while you think, or sketch a scene from your story.

Now it's your turn! Continue the story in your own words on the next page!

Adventure: Story Starter #8

Title:_____

Tip: Writing your story first can help you find a title that really matches what happens in the story. Once you know all the details, you can choose a title that fits it perfectly!

***

Dylan carefully untied the ropes, setting the small boat free from the dock. "Are you sure this is a good idea?" asked his friend Abby, looking uncertain. "Trust me, Abby. The prize will be worth it," Dylan replied. Dylan and Abby planned to catch the biggest crab for the annual seaside contest. They had heard that the largest crabs could be found in the rocky coves far out at sea. With crab traps, bait, and plenty of supplies, they pushed off and set sail.

Brainstorm, doodle, or draw: use this space to jot down your ideas, doodle while you think, or sketch a scene from your story.

Now it's your turn! Continue the story in your own words on the next page!

Chapter 4

Fantasy

When you think of the word 'fantasy,' what do you imagine? Do you imagine magical worlds with wizards and dragons? Or maybe you imagine an enchanted forest where trees and animals speak. Chances are, you've already read fantasy stories or watched fantasy movies. Maybe you even have a favorite. But have you ever thought about what makes fantasy a unique genre?

In the genre of fantasy, anything is possible. Fantasy is a type of make-believe story that breaks the rules of what we know to be real. These stories have places, events, and creatures that can't exist in the real world. This is what makes fantasy stories so exciting to write: the options are limitless!

Secret Ingredients of Fantasy

Let's talk about the characteristics, or 'secret ingredients,' of fantasy stories. These ingredients are often used to write fantasy stories. Each writer may use these ingredients in different combinations, creating a unique 'recipe' for each story.

Let's explore the secret ingredients of fantasy stories:

Magical Elements

Fantasy stories often have magical elements. This can be things like spells, enchantments, potions, or other magical powers.

- **Writing Tip:** Think about a cool magical power you wish you had. Now, give that power to one of your characters. Maybe they can talk to animals, control the weather, or turn invisible.

Imaginary Worlds

Fantasy stories often take place in made-up places like kingdoms, mystical forests, and other realms where real-world rules don't apply.

- **Writing Tip:** Think about what makes your imaginary world unique. Write a short description of one special place in your world. Is it a floating island in the sky? A city made of candy? A secret invisible kingdom? Describe what it looks like and what magical things happen there.

Heroic Characters

The main characters in fantasy stories are often heroes who go on epic quests or adventures. They might be brave knights, clever wizards, or regular kids who discover that they have magical powers.

- **Writing Tip:** Create a hero by thinking about what makes someone brave or clever. Give your hero a challenge to face, like rescuing a friend or finding a lost magical item.

Mythical Creatures

Fantasy worlds are full of creatures like dragons, elves, fairies, and giants. These beings can be friends or enemies of the hero.

- **Writing Tip:** Invent a mythical creature by combining parts of different animals. Maybe it has the wings of an eagle, the tail of a lion, and the head of a dragon. Decide if this creature is a friend or enemy of the hero.

Fantasy Vocabulary

Fantasy stories often use words that you may not see in other genres. Take a look at the list below to discover words frequently used in fantasy stories. Challenge yourself to use a couple of these words when writing your own stories!

Keep in mind that these words may have different uses or definitions in other contexts. These definitions simply reflect their most common uses in the fantasy genre.

Enchanted: Something that has been changed by magic or appears to be under a spell.

- Example sentence: The enchanted forest was filled with glowing flowers that sparkled under the moon.

Quest: A long or difficult journey to reach a special goal.

- Example sentence: The hero sets out on a quest to find the lost treasure.

Mythical: Related to myths or make-believe creatures.

- Example sentence: The land was filled with mythical creatures like unicorns and griffins.

Griffin: A mythical creature with the body of a lion and the head and wings of an eagle.

- Example sentence: The griffin guarded the entrance to the hidden cave.

Elixir: A magical drink believed to heal or give special powers.

- Example sentence: The wizard brewed an elixir that granted the power of flight to anyone who drank it.

Fantasy: Story Starter #1

Title:_____

Tip: Writing your story first can help you find a title that really matches what happens in the story. Once you know all the details, you can choose a title that fits it perfectly!

***

Sam admired his painting. He had used the old paintbrush he found in a box tucked away in his grandmother's attic. He wasn't supposed to go through his grandmother's things, but he didn't think borrowing her paintbrush would be a big deal. He leaned in to look closer at the creature he had painted next to a tall tree with silver leaves. Squinting his eyes and getting his face so close that his nose almost touched the canvas, he gasped. The creature looked directly back at him and smiled.

Brainstorm, doodle, or draw: use this space to jot down your ideas, doodle while you think, or sketch a scene from your story.

Now it's your turn! Continue the story in your own words on the next page!

Fantasy: Story Starter #2

Title:_____

Tip: Writing your story first can help you find a title that really matches what happens in the story. Once you know all the details, you can choose a title that fits it perfectly!

***

Ellara was the only one of her kind who liked to swim & dive in the ocean. The rest of the woodland elves in her community often scolded her for venturing beyond their forest borders. But Ellara loved to dive and didn't care what everyone else thought. She waded into the cool ocean, the full moon just beginning to rise. As she waded further, something caught her eye. She looked closer, shocked. Under the moonlight, a shimmering golden door emerged from the water.

Brainstorm, doodle, or draw: use this space to jot down your ideas, doodle while you think, or sketch a scene from your story.

Now it's your turn! Continue the story in your own words on the next page!

Fantasy: Story Starter #3

Title:_____

Tip: Writing your story first can help you find a title that really matches what happens in the story. Once you know all the details, you can choose a title that fits it perfectly!

***

"Welcome to Mystic Crumbs," an elderly woman with twinkling eyes greeted Felix. He'd heard rumors about this place, that the baked goods were somehow enchanted. He'd begged his parents to take him, but they forbade him from ever stepping foot in the bakery. Now, here he was on his own, coins in hand ready to buy a glowing chocolate croissant.

Brainstorm, doodle, or draw: use this space to jot down your ideas, doodle while you think, or sketch a scene from your story.

Now it's your turn! Continue the story in your own words on the next page!

Fantasy: Story Starter #4

Title:_____

Tip: Writing your story first can help you find a title that really matches what happens in the story. Once you know all the details, you can choose a title that fits it perfectly!

***

Marcy walked around her neighborhood, feeling bored. No other kids were out and she wished she had something more fun to do. Just as she was about to go home, she spotted a shiny green and purple ticket on the ground. She bent down to pick it up. But the moment her fingers touched the ticket, the world spun around her. She felt herself being transported, but she had no idea where she was going.

Brainstorm, doodle, or draw: use this space to jot down your ideas, doodle while you think, or sketch a scene from your story.

Now it's your turn! Continue the story in your own words on the next page!

Fantasy: Story Starter #5

Title:_____

Tip: Writing your story first can help you find a title that really matches what happens in the story. Once you know all the details, you can choose a title that fits it perfectly!

***

Thunder boomed overhead. Jason rushed to put on his raincoat and grabbed his backpack. It was finally happening again. Two months ago, he'd taken a shortcut through the woods to get home during a storm. That's when he discovered it: a mysterious market that seemed to appear out of nowhere. He soon discovered that the market only appeared during thunderstorms. His friends didn't believe him. This time, he was going to prove it. They were going with him. Jason knew his friends would be shocked by what they would find at the market.

Brainstorm, doodle, or draw: use this space to jot down your ideas, doodle while you think, or sketch a scene from your story.

Now it's your turn! Continue the story in your own words on the next page!

Fantasy: Story Starter #6

Title:_____

Tip: Writing your story first can help you find a title that really matches what happens in the story. Once you know all the details, you can choose a title that fits it perfectly!

***

Zara raced out of the front gate. She was going to be in big trouble. Her griffin, Emberclaw, had gotten loose again.

Brainstorm, doodle, or draw: use this space to jot down your ideas, doodle while you think, or sketch a scene from your story.

Now it's your turn! Continue the story in your own words on the next page!

Fantasy: Story Starter #7

Title:_____

Tip: Writing your story first can help you find a title that really matches what happens in the story. Once you know all the details, you can choose a title that fits it perfectly!

***

This wasn't the first time something odd had happened at the Whispering Pines Library, but it was the weirdest. While browsing the shelves, Ethan noticed a book on the top shelf that seemed to be glowing. He stretched on his tiptoes and pulled it down. Suddenly, the bookshelf shifted and revealed a hidden door. Ethan's heart was pounding. He pushed the door open and found himself at the top of a spiral staircase.

Brainstorm, doodle, or draw: use this space to jot down your ideas, doodle while you think, or sketch a scene from your story.

Now it's your turn! Continue the story in your own words on the next page!

Fantasy: Story Starter #8

Title:_____

Tip: Writing your story first can help you find a title that really matches what happens in the story. Once you know all the details, you can choose a title that fits it perfectly!

***

Maxine stood at the edge of the forest. Her hands were shaking. She was about to do something that nobody had done in years. She was going to talk to the forest giants. Maxine knew it was dangerous, but she had no choice. She needed their help.

Brainstorm, doodle, or draw: use this space to jot down your ideas, doodle while you think, or sketch a scene from your story.

Now it's your turn! Continue the story in your own words on the next page!

Chapter 5

Survival Stories

Imagine being stuck in a wild jungle, on a deserted island, or lost in a scorching desert. No phone, no map, and no easy way out. Sounds like a wild adventure, right? This is what survival stories are all about. Characters in survival stories must use their smarts, courage, and strength to stay alive in tough places. These stories are not just about staying alive but also about discovering inner strength and resilience. Survival stories are thrilling because they push characters to face their fears and make tough decisions. These stories teach us about the human spirit, teamwork, and the will to survive against all odds.

Secret Ingredients of Survival Stories

Let's talk about the characteristics, or 'secret ingredients,' of survival stories. These ingredients are often used to make survival stories interesting. Each survival story might use these ingredients in different ways, creating a unique 'recipe' for each story.

Let's explore the secret ingredients of survival stories:

Limited Resources

In survival stories, characters often have to make do with very little. This might mean finding food, water, or shelter with whatever is available around them.

- **Writing Tip:** Imagine your character is stranded with only a few items in their backpack. What do they have, and how do they use these items to survive? Think creatively about how everyday objects can become lifesavers.

Harsh Environments

Survival stories are set in challenging and dangerous places. This can be places like dense forests, high mountains, stormy oceans, or barren deserts. These environments test the characters' abilities to adapt.

- **Writing Tip:** Picture a place where you would find it hard to survive. Write a description of this harsh environment. Is it a frozen landscape or a humid jungle?

Physical Challenges

Characters in survival stories often face physical obstacles. This might mean climbing steep cliffs, swimming across rivers, or enduring extreme weather.

- **Writing Tip:** Make your character face a physical challenge, like climbing a tree to escape an animal or hiking in a blizzard. Write about how they overcome this obstacle.

Learning to Adapt

In survival stories, characters need to learn new skills to stay alive. They have to be quick thinkers and use what's around them to help.

- **Writing Tip:** Think about a skill your character needs to survive, like building a fire, finding food, or making a shelter. Show how this skill helps them survive.

Self-Reliance & Teamwork

Some survival stories are about one person, while others are about a group working together. Characters often have to rely on themselves and each other to get through tough situations.

- **Writing Tip:** Decide if your story will have one survivor or a group. If it's a group, show how they help each other to overcome challenges. If it's one person, show how they use their inner strength and cleverness. Write a scene that shows how they survive.

Survival Story Vocabulary

Survival stories often use words that you may not see in other genres. Here are some words that are often used in survival stories. Challenge yourself to use a couple of these words when writing your own stories!

Keep in mind that these words may have other uses or definitions in other contexts. These definitions simply reflect their most common uses in the survival story genre.

Wilderness: Any wild place in nature where no people live.
- Example sentence: After the plane crash, the three survivors had to learn to survive in the wilderness.

Forage: To search for food and other supplies.
- Example sentence: The kids had to forage for berries and nuts to survive in the wild.

Isolation: Being completely alone.
- Example sentence: Being isolated made it hard for Kelly to think of good things when she was lost in the woods.

Ration: A small amount of resources like food or a way to split up the resources for each person
- Example sentence: With only two boxes of granola bars, the group decided to ration one bar each day to make their food supply last longer.

Adapt: Changing to fit new environments or events.
- Example sentence: Every survivor has to adapt to their environment to stay healthy and safe.

Survival Stories: Story Starter #1

Title:_____

Tip: Writing your story first can help you find a title that really matches what happens in the story. Once you know all the details, you can choose a title that fits it perfectly!

***

Cody and his friend Tom were now alone on the mountain, the wind howling through the trees like a pack of wolves. Their hiking group had vanished into the thick fog that rolled in with the sudden storm. Cody glanced at Tom, his heart pounding in his chest. "We need to find shelter," Cody shouted over the roar of the storm. Tom nodded, his eyes wide with fear. "But where?"

Brainstorm, doodle, or draw: use this space to jot down your ideas, doodle while you think, or sketch a scene from your story.

Now it's your turn! Continue the story in your own words on the next page!

Survival Stories: Story Starter #2

Title:_____

Tip: Writing your story first can help you find a title that really matches what happens in the story. Once you know all the details, you can choose a title that fits it perfectly!

***

Laura was busy studying ice samples in the Arctic near her research facility. She was farther away than usual but planned to head back soon. Suddenly, she felt the ice shift under her feet. The ice cracked loudly. Before she could do anything, the piece she was standing on broke off and floated into the ocean. Her heart pounded. She was stuck on a floating island of ice with only her emergency supplies.

Brainstorm, doodle, or draw: use this space to jot down your ideas, doodle while you think, or sketch a scene from your story.

Now it's your turn! Continue the story in your own words on the next page!

Survival Stories: Story Starter #3

Title:_____

Tip: Writing your story first can help you find a title that really matches what happens in the story. Once you know all the details, you can choose a title that fits it perfectly!

***

Hudson opened his eyes to the sound of waves crashing on the shore. He groaned and sat up, realizing he was on a sandy beach surrounded by debris from the plane crash. He had survived, but now he was alone on a deserted island with no supplies. Hudson knew he had to adapt quickly to survive.

Brainstorm, doodle, or draw: use this space to jot down your ideas, doodle while you think, or sketch a scene from your story.

Now it's your turn! Continue the story in your own words on the next page!

Survival Stories: Story Starter #4

Title:_____

Tip: Writing your story first can help you find a title that really matches what happens in the story. Once you know all the details, you can choose a title that fits it perfectly!

***

A loud rumble echoed around Sadie and her team. The ceiling of the cave was collapsing, trapping them inside. Dust filled the air, and they were plunged into darkness. Sadie could hear the fluttering of bats overhead. She took a deep breath. "I can't panic," she thought. "I'm the leader."

Brainstorm, doodle, or draw: use this space to jot down your ideas, doodle while you think, or sketch a scene from your story.

Now it's your turn! Continue the story in your own words on the next page!

Survival Stories: Story Starter #5

Title:_____

Tip: Writing your story first can help you find a title that really matches what happens in the story. Once you know all the details, you can choose a title that fits it perfectly!

***

Asher and his dog Benny were excited to reach the big sledding hill on the other side of the woods. He had his sled, gloves, hat, and a small bag of trail mix. He didn't plan to be out long. But as they walked, a sudden snowstorm hit, and soon they were lost in the thick, swirling snow. Asher looked around, trying to find his way, but everything was white and confusing.

Brainstorm, doodle, or draw: use this space to jot down your ideas, doodle while you think, or sketch a scene from your story.

Now it's your turn! Continue the story in your own words on the next page!

Survival Stories: Story Starter #6

Title:_____

Tip: Writing your story first can help you find a title that really matches what happens in the story. Once you know all the details, you can choose a title that fits it perfectly!

***

Emery and Jade were out on their boat, collecting lobster pots. Suddenly, they realized they were running out of fuel. They tried to turn back, but the engine sputtered and died, leaving them stuck. The current started pulling them deeper out to sea. Emery turned to Jade with worry in her eyes. "We don't have any cell service out here," she said.

Brainstorm, doodle, or draw: use this space to jot down your ideas, doodle while you think, or sketch a scene from your story.

Now it's your turn! Continue the story in your own words on the next page!

Survival Stories: Story Starter #7

Title:_____

Tip: Writing your story first can help you find a title that really matches what happens in the story. Once you know all the details, you can choose a title that fits it perfectly!

***

The thick foliage surrounded Nathan and Wren, and soon they were completely lost. They should never have ventured away from their tour guide in the Amazon jungle. Strange noises echoed through the trees, reminding them of all the dangerous animals the guide had mentioned. Nathan's heart pounded as he whispered to Wren, "We need to stay calm and find our way back."

Brainstorm, doodle, or draw: use this space to jot down your ideas, doodle while you think, or sketch a scene from your story.

Now it's your turn! Continue the story in your own words on the next page!

Survival Stories: Story Starter #8

Title:_____

Tip: Writing your story first can help you find a title that really matches what happens in the story. Once you know all the details, you can choose a title that fits it perfectly!

***

The blackout had knocked out all electricity in the city. Angel and Jordan had waited days for their parents to return home, but they still weren't back. They peered outside the window at the chaos unfolding in the streets. They didn't want to go out there, but they needed food and water.

Brainstorm, doodle, or draw: use this space to jot down your ideas, doodle while you think, or sketch a scene from your story.

Now it's your turn! Continue the story in your own words on the next page!

Chapter 6

Superheroes

Have you ever imagined what it would be like to have superpowers? Maybe you've thought about being able to fly super fast or pictured having the strength to lift a car with one hand. Superhero stories are all about characters with amazing powers you won't find in the real world. Superheroes have powers that don't exist in reality, but these stories often take place in a real-world setting. This is a big part of what makes superhero stories so exciting. They allow you to imagine what it would be like if superheroes existed in everyday life.

Secret Ingredients of Superhero Stories

Let's talk about the characteristics, or 'secret ingredients,' of superhero stories. These ingredients are often used to make superhero stories interesting. Each superhero story might use these ingredients in different ways, creating a unique 'recipe' for each story.

Let's explore the secret ingredients of superhero stories:

Superpowers

All superheroes has some kind of superpower or extraordinary ability. This can be things like super strength, flight, invisibility, or the power to control elements like fire or ice.

- **Writing Tip:** Think about a superpower you wish you had. Now, give that power to one of your characters. Maybe they can read minds, run faster than the speed of light, or manipulate time.

Secret Identities

Many superheroes have secret identities to protect themselves and their loved ones. They might be ordinary people by day and superheroes by night.

- **Writing Tip:** Create a secret identity for your superhero. What is their everyday life like? Are they a student, a scientist, or a reporter? Think about how they keep their superhero identity hidden.

Villains

Every superhero needs a villain to challenge them. Villains can be evil masterminds, powerful creatures, or even former friends turned enemies.

- **Writing Tip:** Create a villain with a unique motive and powers. Maybe they seek revenge, want to take over the world, or have a grudge against the hero.

Sidekicks & Allies

Superheroes often have sidekicks or allies who help them in their adventures. These characters can provide support, comic relief, or additional skills.

- **Writing Tip:** Create a sidekick or ally for your superhero. What abilities or skills do they bring to the team? Are they tech-savvy, a skilled fighter, or have their own power?

Amazing Fights and Battles

Superhero stories are filled with action-packed scenes of heroes battling villains. These epic fights often involve big risks and dramatic confrontations.

- **Writing Tip:** Plan an exciting battle between your hero and villain. Think about the setting, superpowers, and challenges. Describe the action in a way that keeps readers on the edge of their seats.

Superhero Story Vocabulary

Superhero stories often use words that you may not see in other genres. Here are some words that are often used in superhero stories. Challenge yourself to use a couple of these words when writing your own stories!

Keep in mind that these words may have other uses or definitions in other contexts. These definitions simply reflect their most common uses in the superhero genre.

Alias: A superhero's secret name or persona.
- Example sentence: Mrs. Loomis, the school librarian, keeps her superhero alias hidden during the day. At night, she puts on her costume and fights the evil Book Worm.

Gadgets: Tech devices or tools that a superhero (or anyone) uses.
- Example sentence: The hero straps his gadgets to his power belt: a grappling hook, a shrink ray, and the blade of justice.

Transformation: To change from one thing to another or change how you look.
- Example sentence: When duty calls, Major Boom makes his transformation from a bus driver to a superhero.

Nemesis: An enemy who always fights against the superhero.
- Example sentence: For years, The Splash has fought against his nemesis, Dr. Crab, who always tries to stop his efforts to protect the beach town.

Sacrifice: Giving up something valuable to do good for others.
- Example sentence: The hero sacrifices his time and energy to protect the people of the city at all costs.

Superheroes: Story Starter #1

Title:_____

Tip: Writing your story first can help you find a title that really matches what happens in the story. Once you know all the details, you can choose a title that fits it perfectly!

***

When twins Joshua and Gabriel found out they could turn invisible, they didn't think it would lead to trouble. But now, they're in a big mess.

Brainstorm, doodle, or draw: use this space to jot down your ideas, doodle while you think, or sketch a scene from your story.

Now it's your turn! Continue the story in your own words on the next page!

Superheroes: Story Starter #2

Title:_____

Tip: Writing your story first can help you find a title that really matches what happens in the story. Once you know all the details, you can choose a title that fits it perfectly!

***

Farah peeked out from behind the library shelves. She had fallen asleep while reading, and now the library was closed. The lights were still on, so she knew Miss Alice, the librarian, must be there. Farah spotted Miss Alice pushing a cart of books towards a shelf. Just as Farah was about to call out, she watched in amazement as Miss Alice pointed at a book. The book floated into the air and landed neatly on the shelf. "Telekinesis!" Farah thought, shocked.

Brainstorm, doodle, or draw: use this space to jot down your ideas, doodle while you think, or sketch a scene from your story.

Now it's your turn! Continue the story in your own words on the next page!

Superheroes: Story Starter #3

Title:_____

Tip: Writing your story first can help you find a title that really matches what happens in the story. Once you know all the details, you can choose a title that fits it perfectly!

***

Scott felt relieved to be home after weeks of recovery in the hospital. He'd been hurt in a car accident and broken a few bones. He stood in front of the bathroom mirror. "I wish I didn't have this ugly scar on my face," he thought. Just then, the scar disappeared. Scott gasped. He couldn't believe it. As a joke, Scott tried again. "I wish I looked like a superhero," he thought. He didn't think anything would happen, but to his surprise, he suddenly transformed.

Brainstorm, doodle, or draw: use this space to jot down your ideas, doodle while you think, or sketch a scene from your story.

Now it's your turn! Continue the story in your own words on the next page!

Superheroes: Story Starter #4

Title:_____

Tip: Writing your story first can help you find a title that really matches what happens in the story. Once you know all the details, you can choose a title that fits it perfectly!

***

It had only been a few days since Layla discovered she could walk through people's dreams. She found out by accident and didn't know how to control it yet. One night, while exploring her ability, she stumbled into a nightmare. She noticed someone in the dream who didn't seem to belong. "Does this person have the same power as me?" she thought. As she got closer, she realized this mysterious figure was creating the nightmare on purpose.

Brainstorm, doodle, or draw: use this space to jot down your ideas, doodle while you think, or sketch a scene from your story.

Now it's your turn! Continue the story in your own words on the next page!

Superheroes: Story Starter #5

Title: _____

Tip: Writing your story first can help you find a title that really matches what happens in the story. Once you know all the details, you can choose a title that fits it perfectly!

***

Aaron and his tech-savvy hamster sidekick, Gizmo, were out for a regular patrol in the city when they heard a loud crash. They rushed to the scene and saw a thief stealing a valuable gem from the museum. Aaron took to the skies, flying fast to catch up.

Brainstorm, doodle, or draw: use this space to jot down your ideas, doodle while you think, or sketch a scene from your story.

Now it's your turn! Continue the story in your own words on the next page!

Superheroes: Story Starter #6

Title:_____

Tip: Writing your story first can help you find a title that really matches what happens in the story. Once you know all the details, you can choose a title that fits it perfectly!

***

Willow hated that she had the ability to read minds. Her parents called it a gift but didn't feel that way. They didn't know what it was like to hear everyone's true thoughts. Most of the time, Willow blocked out the noise with headphones. Today, though, her headphones had stopped working. She sat outside waiting for her mom to pick her up when she overheard someone thinking about a plan to steal from the local animal shelter.

Brainstorm, doodle, or draw: use this space to jot down your ideas, doodle while you think, or sketch a scene from your story.

Now it's your turn! Continue the story in your own words on the next page!

Superheroes: Story Starter #7

Title:_____

Tip: Writing your story first can help you find a title that really matches what happens in the story. Once you know all the details, you can choose a title that fits it perfectly!

***

Billy came from a family of superheroes, each with their own incredible powers. But they had to hide their identities from the rest of the world. Every day was a challenge, keeping his powers a secret while living a normal life. One afternoon, while playing soccer in the park, Billy saw a car speeding towards his friends. Without thinking, he used his super speed to save them. Shocked and amazed, his friends stared at him. "Billy, how did you do that?" they asked.

Brainstorm, doodle, or draw: use this space to jot down your ideas, doodle while you think, or sketch a scene from your story.

Now it's your turn! Continue the story in your own words on the next page!

Superheroes: Story Starter #8

Title:_____

Tip: Writing your story first can help you find a title that really matches what happens in the story. Once you know all the details, you can choose a title that fits it perfectly!

***

One day, while playing in the backyard, Maggie and her friend Rachel were bitten by a strange, glowing moth. At first, nothing seemed different. But that night, as it got dark, Maggie and Rachel felt something strange. They began to lift off the ground. Soon, they were both flying.

Brainstorm, doodle, or draw: use this space to jot down your ideas, doodle while you think, or sketch a scene from your story.

Now it's your turn! Continue the story in your own words on the next page!

Chapter 7

Animal Stories

What would it be like if animals could speak, think, and act just like people? That's what animal stories are all about. These stories give animals realistic human traits (like the ability to speak) to create unique characters and adventures. Some animal stories have realistic settings and others have more magical or fantastical settings. Many animal stories teach us about friendship, bravery, and the importance of nature.

Secret Ingredients of Animal Stories

Let's talk about the characteristics, or 'secret ingredients,' of animal stories. These ingredients are often used to make animal stories interesting. Each animal story might use these ingredients in different ways, creating a unique 'recipe' for each story.

Let's explore the secret ingredients of animal stories:

Talking Animals

In many animal stories, the animals can speak and think like humans. This lets us see the world from their perspective.

- **Writing Tip:** Imagine if your pet could talk! What would they say? Create a character based on your favorite animal and give them a unique voice and personality.

Journeys & Adventures

Animal stories often feature exciting journeys and adventures. These can be within the animal's natural habitat or in an entirely imagined world.

- **Writing Tip:** Think of an adventure your animal character could go on. Maybe they need to find a new home, rescue a friend, or explore a mysterious forest.

Animal Friendships

Friendships between animals, or between animals and humans, are a common theme. These stories often explore the themes of loyalty, trust, and teamwork.

- **Writing Tip:** Create a pair of unlikely friends, like a cat and a dog, or a bird and a fish. Think about how they overcome their differences to work together.

Unique Animal Abilities

Animals have unique skills and abilities that can be interesting to include in your story. This could be things like a cheetah's speed, an owl's night vision, or a dolphin's intelligence.

- **Writing Tip:** Choose an animal and think about their special abilities. How can these abilities help them solve problems or overcome challenges in your story?

Imaginative Settings

Animal stories can take place in many different kinds of places, like a dense jungle, a vast ocean, a cozy barn, or a busy city. The setting is important because it helps shape the story.

- **Writing Tip:** Describe the world your animal characters live in. Is it a magical forest, a lively city, or a calm countryside? How does this setting impact your characters? For example, imagine a pigeon who lives in the city and has to navigate through traffic and skyscrapers to deliver an important message.

Animal Story Vocabulary

Animal stories often use words that you may not see in other genres. Here are some words that are often used in animal stories. Challenge yourself to use a couple of these words when writing your own stories!

Keep in mind that these words may have other uses or definitions in other contexts. These definitions simply reflect their most common uses in the animal story genre.

Habitat: Natural environment where a specific animal lives.
- Example sentence: The skunks would not leave their forest habitat, not even to help the turtle find his lost family.

Nocturnal: Active at night.
- Example sentence: Since Harry the hedgehog is nocturnal, he makes an excellent DJ for the midnight mouse party.

Camouflage: The ability to blend in with the surroundings.
- Example sentence: On the secret spy mission in the deep sea, the octopus's camouflage skills helped save the day.

Instinct: A natural pattern of behavior for animals.
- Example sentence: The squirrel's natural instinct told them that a predator lurked nearby, so they raised the alarm before darting back to the high branches.

Territory: An area that an animal considers their own and will protect
- Example sentence: The lions patrolled their territory so no hyenas could get inside and threaten their cubs.

Animal Stories: Story Starter #1

Title:_____

Tip: Writing your story first can help you find a title that really matches what happens in the story. Once you know all the details, you can choose a title that fits it perfectly!

***

High up in the forest canopy, the annual flying squirrel race was about to begin. Squeaky, the smallest but fastest squirrel, tightened his flight suit. He glanced nervously at his competitors. Suddenly, a shadow swept over the starting line. The chatter of excitement turned to hushed whispers. It was Ollie, the notorious barn owl known for causing trouble.

Brainstorm, doodle, or draw: use this space to jot down your ideas, doodle while you think, or sketch a scene from your story.

Now it's your turn! Continue the story in your own words on the next page!

Animal Stories: Story Starter #2

Title:_____

Tip: Writing your story first can help you find a title that really matches what happens in the story. Once you know all the details, you can choose a title that fits it perfectly!

***

On the icy shores of the arctic, Frosty the fox, Pippin the puffin, and Sammy the seal always stayed close to their homes. One day, a fierce blizzard swept across the land. It caught the trio off guard and blew them far away. They ended up miles away from their familiar territories.

Brainstorm, doodle, or draw: use this space to jot down your ideas, doodle while you think, or sketch a scene from your story.

Now it's your turn! Continue the story in your own words on the next page!

Animal Stories: Story Starter #3

Title:_____

Tip: Writing your story first can help you find a title that really matches what happens in the story. Once you know all the details, you can choose a title that fits it perfectly!

***

In the heart of the dense forest, the Silvermoon wolf pack gathered under the full moon. Their leader, Koda, felt something was wrong. The rival Shadowclaw pack had been coming into their territory. Tensions were rising. One night, during a patrol, the Silvermoon scouts found strange tracks leading toward their den.

Brainstorm, doodle, or draw: use this space to jot down your ideas, doodle while you think, or sketch a scene from your story.

Now it's your turn! Continue the story in your own words on the next page!

Animal Stories: Story Starter #4

Title:_____

Tip: Writing your story first can help you find a title that really matches what happens in the story. Once you know all the details, you can choose a title that fits it perfectly!

***

In the lush, green rainforest, Rocco the red-eyed tree frog lived a peaceful life. One day, a mysterious illness began spreading among the animals. The wise old parrot, Maya, told Rocco about a magical flower deep in the heart of the jungle that could cure the sickness. Rocco knew he had to find it, even though the journey would be dangerous.

Brainstorm, doodle, or draw: use this space to jot down your ideas, doodle while you think, or sketch a scene from your story.

Now it's your turn! Continue the story in your own words on the next page!

Animal Stories: Story Starter #5

Title:_____

Tip: Writing your story first can help you find a title that really matches what happens in the story. Once you know all the details, you can choose a title that fits it perfectly!

***

In a busy city neighborhood, a group of cats secretly formed a spy group. Led by Shadow, a clever tabby, they kept the peace and solved mysteries when humans weren't looking. One night, Shadow discovered a strange message scratched into the sidewalk.

Brainstorm, doodle, or draw: use this space to jot down your ideas, doodle while you think, or sketch a scene from your story.

Now it's your turn! Continue the story in your own words on the next page!

Animal Stories: Story Starter #6

Title:_____

Tip: Writing your story first can help you find a title that really matches what happens in the story. Once you know all the details, you can choose a title that fits it perfectly!

***

In a cozy living room, a bright green parakeet named Kiwi lived in a large, comfortable cage. One day, while his owner was out, Kiwi noticed the cage door had been left open. Curiosity got the best of him, and he fluttered out.

Brainstorm, doodle, or draw: use this space to jot down your ideas, doodle while you think, or sketch a scene from your story.

Now it's your turn! Continue the story in your own words on the next page!

Animal Stories: Story Starter #7

Title:_____

Tip: Writing your story first can help you find a title that really matches what happens in the story. Once you know all the details, you can choose a title that fits it perfectly!

***

In the deep blue ocean, a pod of orca whales swam together, led by the wise elder, Kai. One day, while playing near a deep trench, they encountered a massive shadow rising from the depths.

Brainstorm, doodle, or draw: use this space to jot down your ideas, doodle while you think, or sketch a scene from your story.

Now it's your turn! Continue the story in your own words on the next page!

Animal Stories: Story Starter #8

Title:_____

Tip: Writing your story first can help you find a title that really matches what happens in the story. Once you know all the details, you can choose a title that fits it perfectly!

***

A flock of migrating geese flew in perfect formation, led by the eldest goose, Scout. They were on their way to their winter home when a sudden storm blew in, scattering the flock in all directions.

Brainstorm, doodle, or draw: use this space to jot down your ideas, doodle while you think, or sketch a scene from your story.

Now it's your turn! Continue the story in your own words on the next page!

Made in the USA
Las Vegas, NV
04 October 2024

96316285R00081